Publishing Credits

Dona Herweck Rice, *Editor-in-Chief*
Lee Aucoin, *Creative Director*
Kristy Stark, M.A.Ed., *Senior Editor*
Torrey Maloof, *Editor*
Kristine Magnien, M.S.Ed., *Associate Education Editor*
Neri Garcia, *Senior Designer*
Stephanie Reid, *Photo Researcher*
Rachelle Cracchiolo, M.S.Ed., *Publisher*

Image Credits

cover: Thinkstock; all other images from Shutterstock.

Teacher Created Materials

5301 Oceanus Drive
Huntington Beach, CA 92649-1030
http://www.tcmpub.com
ISBN 978-1-4333-4764-1
© 2013 Teacher Created Materials, Inc.
Made in China
Nordica.072017.CA21700826

Table of Contents

Dear Family,

This is an exciting year for your first grader! Many children become readers during first grade. They begin to master useful math skills that will serve them well for life. They are ready for more formal instruction in topics such as science and social studies. They also learn to socialize with a larger pool of children and adults.

You've been your child's primary teacher since the beginning. Now, your child's teacher will play a big role in your child's day. Don't be surprised if your first grader loves his or her teacher! This is the ideal time to build a partnership with the teacher to ensure a love of learning. You have already begun to develop many important skills as your child's first and most important teacher!

This parent guide will give you even more parent-tested ideas. From tips for organizing school materials to strategies for incorporating learning opportunities into your busy day— you are sure to find some ideas that are just right for you.

One last thought...

Keep in mind that you are setting the stage for habits that will help your child for the rest of his or her life. This will be a busy and important year, but don't forget to have fun along the way!

Forming
Routines at Home

Let's face it, days are pretty busy. There's nothing worse than trying to find that permission slip or homework minutes before the bus or carpool arrives.

We want our children to be self-sufficient. First grade is a good time for your child to take on more responsibility.

Try these ideas to prevent frantic mornings.

In- and Out-Boxes

When your child gets home from school, have him or her put all school papers into the in-box. Once everything is finished or signed, the papers that go back to school can be placed into the out-box.

Pack It Up

Collect the papers from the out-box and have your child put them in his or her backpack the night before.

Chores

Have your child perform a regular chore, such as making the bed or emptying the trash.

Schedule

Plan a schedule together. The schedule can include playing, chores, snack, homework, reading time, and bedtime. Post a schedule for your child and any caregivers to see.

SCHEDULE

4:00	Snack
4:30	Piano practice
5:00	Set the table, feed the dog
5:30	Dinner
6:30	Homework and reading time
7:00	Free time (after homework)
7:30	Get ready for bed

One last thought...

Use a timer to help your child keep to the schedule.

Homework
Habits

Most young children love school. Make the most of this love of learning by forming good work habits and creating a practical work environment. One way to do this is to establish a routine of working quietly for 15 minutes a day.

Work 15 minutes

No TV

Prepare a work station

These tips will help your first grader form good work habits.

Workstation

Prepare a workstation with paper, pencils, crayons, a ruler, scissors, and a children's dictionary, if possible.

Keep It Quiet

Turn off the television and try to keep the room quiet when your child is working.

A Helping Hand

Be ready to offer help when it's needed. Don't help your child too much, but don't let your him or her get frustrated.

Finish the 15

If your child finishes early, have him or her read picture books until the 15 minutes are up.

Stick to the Routine

Even if your child doesn't have homework, it is important that he or she still works quietly for 15 minutes to help set the routine.

$$\begin{array}{r} 6 \\ +\ 9 \\ \hline \end{array}$$

One last thought...

Spend five minutes a day practicing skills with flash cards. Flash cards with addition and subtraction or flash cards with sight words such as *when, then, the,* and *there* can be made or purchased.

Starting Family Conversations

Do you remember how exciting it was when your child said *mama* or *dada* for the first time? Now, you may long for a bit of peace and quiet! However, talking with your first grader is one of the best things you can do to build your child's vocabulary skills.

Here are some questions that will get your child talking.

What new thing did you learn at school today?

Here are more conversation starters.

Who did something funny? What was it?

What did your teacher read to you?

What was the best part of the day?

One last thought...

Talk while in the car, when buying groceries, when on a walk, and during a snack. Sharing stories at dinner is also a great routine to start.

Sleep Suggestions

Did you know that without the right amount of sleep, your first grader will have a hard time focusing and learning in school? Plus, without enough sleep, your child may be grouchy! And who wants that?

The chart below shows how much sleep children need.

Age	Sleep Needed
1–3 years	12–14 hours
3–5 years	11–13 hours
5–12 years	10–11 hours

Here are some tips for making sure your first grader gets enough sleep.

Time for Bed
Make sure your child goes to bed at the same time every night.

Keep It Quiet
Turn off the television and try to keep the room quiet when your child is sleeping.

Staying the Same
Keep the bedtime environment (e.g., light, temperature, quiet) the same all night long.

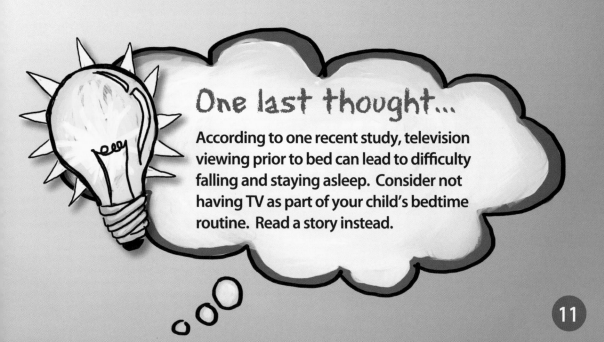

One last thought...
According to one recent study, television viewing prior to bed can lead to difficulty falling and staying asleep. Consider not having TV as part of your child's bedtime routine. Read a story instead.

Top 10
Things Your First Grader
Needs to Know

1. **Read grade-level books** with ease and understanding

2. **Read and spell** sight words

3. **Write complete sentences** with correct capitalization and punctuation

4. **Count**, read, and write to 100

5. **Addition and subtraction** facts up to 20

6. Simple two-digit **addition and subtraction** problems (without regrouping)

7. **Five senses** (sight, taste, touch, sound, and smell) to observe and describe things

8. **Living things** and their habitats

9. **Rules and responsibilities** of being a good citizen

10. **The United States' holidays and symbols**

Words
on the Go

Most children learn more than 1,000 words per year before they start school. Having a good vocabulary pays off throughout life. Luckily, we live in a world full of words. This makes learning new words fun and easy.

These word games will help your first grader build his or her vocabulary.

I Spy
"I spy a word that starts with the letter A."

Find the Food
"Find the food spelled E-G-G."

I'm Thinking of...
"I'm thinking of a fruit that is green."

Rhyme Time
"I'm thinking of a word that rhymes with cat."

One last thought...

Kids Learn! Sight Words 1–300 is a great app for sight word practice and fun. It's available for some devices.

Reading
Aloud

You have probably read countless picture books to your child. Reading aloud is one of the best practices to continue, even if for just a few minutes each day. It is important for your first grader to hear you read aloud with expression and fluency. It is also important for your child to see you read for pleasure. By reading in front of your child, you will model the importance of reading.

These activities will help improve your child's reading.

Make It a Play
Turn your child's favorite book into a play. Have your first grader act out the story as you read it aloud.

Stories on the Go
Borrow audio books from the library and listen to them in the car.

Read and Work
Take turns doing chores and reading aloud. One person can read aloud while the other does the chore.

Reading Long Distance
Have your child read a story aloud to a distant relative via video chat or telephone.

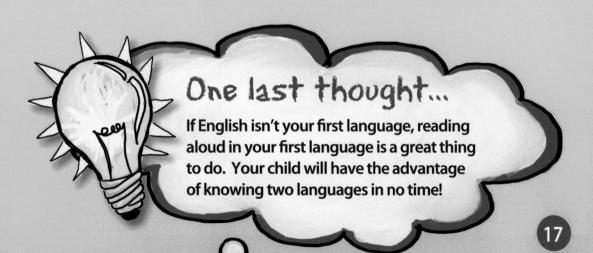

One last thought...
If English isn't your first language, reading aloud in your first language is a great thing to do. Your child will have the advantage of knowing two languages in no time!

Building
a Library

Thousands of children's books are published each year. There are many ways for finding books to help you build a library at home. You probably remember authors from your childhood that you want to share with your child. Your child probably has a few favorite authors, too!

Here are some great books for your first grader.

- *The Cat and the Hat* by Dr. Seuss
- *Stellaluna* by Janell Cannon
- *Click, Clack, Moo* by Doreen Cronin
- *Go, Dog, Go* by P.D. Eastman
- *I Wish I Had Duck Feet* by Theo. LeSieg
- *Hi! Fly Guy* by Tedd Arnold
- *Owl at Home* by Arnold Lobel
- *Pancakes for Breakfast* by Tomie dePaola
- *Wouldn't You?* by John Ciardi
- *Be Myself* by Eloise Greenfield

Here are some ideas for how to find books.

- Library book sales
- Garage sales
- Sales at bookstores
- Swap books with neighbors

One last thought...

Build a library corner together in your home. It can be as simple as a set of shelves with some pillows and good lighting in a quiet place.

Spelling
and Writing Practice

Your first grader will spend a lot of time working on spelling and writing this year. Don't be surprised if letters such as *b* and *d* are reversed or if some letters drift off the lines of the paper. And while many words are easy to spell, others are not. You can help your child by providing paper with wide lines, pencils and erasers, and many opportunities to spell and write.

These ideas will help your first grader have fun with spelling and writing.

Spelling with Magnets
Have your child practice spelling with magnets on the refrigerator.

Spelling with Food

Have your child use letter-shaped cookies to create words.

Writing Cards

Have your child help you write cards for
special events such as birthdays,
weddings, and new babies.

Writing Lists

Have your child help you write your
shopping lists.

Rainbow Spelling

Have your child write spelling words in one
color and then go over each letter with additional
colors until there is a rainbow effect.

Writing Letters

Have your child tell you what he or she wants to write. You write it
and then have your child copy it.

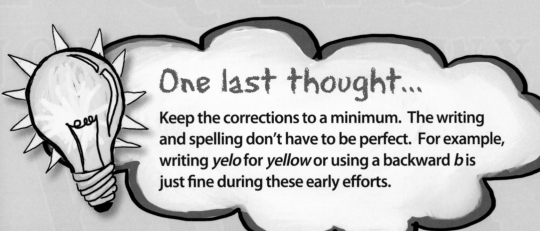

One last thought...

Keep the corrections to a minimum. The writing
and spelling don't have to be perfect. For example,
writing *yelo* for *yellow* or using a backward *b* is
just fine during these early efforts.

Sight Words

Sight words are words that should be identified quickly, without sounding them out. Here is a list that a first grader should know by sight.

I	**the**
a	**see**
to	**my**
and	**go**
is	**are**
for	**he**

have	as
said	was
like	this
of	they
that	you
on	in
with	it
she	at

Math
on the Go

Do you remember learning how to count out change or figuring out how many hours until school gets out? For some, this comes easy. But for most, these skills require practice.

Try these ideas for reinforcing math while on the go.

How many vegetables?
Have your child categorize and count the items in your shopping cart while at the market.

What number is on this bill?
Have your child identify numbers on receipts.

What coin is this?
Have your child close his or her eyes and identify coins by their size and feel.

Can you find the number?
Have your child find numbers on signs and products.

One last thought...

Use any opportunity to count such as telling time, going up stairs, and picking up toys or books.

Math
at Home

Your first grader will be learning addition and subtraction this year. There will be lots of practice on paper at school. You can help your child master addition and subtraction while you are home.

• •

Here are a few ideas on how to turn everyday actions into math problems.

Counting in the Kitchen

"How many apples are there? How many oranges are there? How many apples and oranges do we have in all?"

Baking Math Problems

"This recipe calls for 1 teaspoon each of vanilla, cinnamon, and baking powder. How many teaspoons go into this recipe?"

Laundry Math

"How many socks are yours? How many socks are mine? How many socks do we have in all?"

Recycling Math

"How many cans are there? How many bottles? How many total? If we put the cans in the bin, then how many bottles are left?"

Math Facts
Up to 20

First graders are moving away from counting on their fingers and doing more mental math. Memorizing math facts up to 20 will help improve your child's math skills. Use these math facts on flash cards and play a game to help your child memorize them.

1 + 0 = 1	2 + 0 = 2	3 + 0 = 3	4 + 0 = 4	5 + 0 = 5
1 + 1 = 2	2 + 1 = 3	3 + 1 = 4	4 + 1 = 5	5 + 1 = 6
1 + 2 = 3	2 + 2 = 4	3 + 2 = 5	4 + 2 = 6	5 + 2 = 7
1 + 3 = 4	2 + 3 = 5	3 + 3 = 6	4 + 3 = 7	5 + 3 = 8
1 + 4 = 5	2 + 4 = 6	3 + 4 = 7	4 + 4 = 8	5 + 4 = 9
1 + 5 = 6	2 + 5 = 7	3 + 5 = 8	4 + 5 = 9	5 + 5 = 10
1 + 6 = 7	2 + 6 = 8	3 + 6 = 9	4 + 6 = 10	5 + 6 = 11
1 + 7 = 8	2 + 7 = 9	3 + 7 = 10	4 + 7 = 11	5 + 7 = 12
1 + 8 = 9	2 + 8 = 10	3 + 8 = 11	4 + 8 = 12	5 + 8 = 13
1 + 9 = 10	2 + 9 = 11	3 + 9 = 12	4 + 9 = 13	5 + 9 = 14
1 + 10 = 11	2 + 10 = 12	3 + 10 = 13	4 + 10 = 14	5 + 10 = 15

6 + 0 = 6	7 + 0 = 7	8 + 0 = 8	9 + 0 = 9	10 + 0 = 10
6 + 1 = 7	7 + 1 = 8	8 + 1 = 9	9 + 1 = 10	10 + 1 = 11
6 + 2 = 8	7 + 2 = 9	8 + 2 = 10	9 + 2 = 11	10 + 2 = 12
6 + 3 = 9	7 + 3 = 10	8 + 3 = 11	9 + 3 = 12	10 + 3 = 13
6 + 4 = 10	7 + 4 = 11	8 + 4 = 12	9 + 4 = 13	10 + 4 = 14
6 + 5 = 11	7 + 5 = 12	8 + 5 = 13	9 + 5 = 14	10 + 5 = 15
6 + 6 = 12	7 + 6 = 13	8 + 6 = 14	9 + 6 = 15	10 + 6 = 16
6 + 7 = 13	7 + 7 = 14	8 + 7 = 15	9 + 7 = 16	10 + 7 = 17
6 + 8 = 14	7 + 8 = 15	8 + 8 = 16	9 + 8 = 17	10 + 8 = 18
6 + 9 = 15	7 + 9 = 16	8 + 9 = 17	9 + 9 = 18	10 + 9 = 19
6 + 10 = 16	7 + 10 = 17	8 + 10 = 18	9 + 10 = 19	10 + 10 = 20

Science

All Around

Your first grader has always been a scientist. Curiosity about how things work in the world is natural. During the first grade, your child will be learning about plants, animals, their habitats, the weather, and how to think about investigations and experiments.

These activities will help your child to think scientifically and critically.

Seasonal Talk

When walking to the bus, park, or store, talk about the changing seasons.

Tracking the Weather

Have your child draw a sun, clouds, rain, or snow daily on a calendar to track the weather.

Animal Watching

When outside, take time to notice the animals in your area.
Discuss any animals you see and what they are doing.

Sensing Food

Pick a fruit or vegetable and have
your child describe it using
his or her five senses (sight,
touch, taste, sound, smell).

One last thought...

Enjoy your child's natural interest in all things squishy,
wiggly, and crawly. Even things adults may find
creepy, may fascinate children. You may find you
have a budding scientist in the family.

Social Studies
Skills

Your first grader is learning that there are rules. There are expectations that go with these rules. During this year, he or she will be learning about the world outside of the home and school through social studies.

Help your child develop an awareness of community, history, and diversity with these activities.

Use a Map
When going someplace new, show your child where you'll be going on a map.

Saving Money
Help your child learn about spending and saving by having him or her do chores for money. Set up three jars for spending, saving, and sharing (money for charity).

Symbols

Watch for landmarks such as statues or historical markers. Stop and talk about the person or event.

Family History

Encourage older generations to share their experiences through stories. If possible, videotape the conversations to make a priceless memento.

One last thought...

Use family meetings to solve problems or make group decisions. Each family member can vote. Of course, parents have veto power!

Learning
in the Community

As your first grader becomes more social, you will want to find more group activities for him or her. Your school or community may have many programs. However, constraints of time or money may mean you have to be innovative.

Here are some ideas to help your child be more socially active.

Field Trips
Work out a schedule with a few families in your community to share the responsibility for taking all the kids to a museum or other special place.

Team Sports
Organize sports teams in your community. Team sports such as soccer or T-ball should focus on skills and fun at this age, not winning.

Playground Games

Consider starting a Saturday morning game club. Children from your community can come and play Capture the Flag, Mother May I?, or Four Square.

Talented Friends

Work with friends (or grandparents) with talents and skills to provide enrichment activities. They can help teach arts and crafts, musical instruments, cooking, or even host a reading club.

One last thought...

Strike a balance. Your child will need some time to play, dream, and maybe even get a little bit bored.

Learning
in the Car

Between carpooling and errands, most families spend a lot of time in the car. This is a great time to learn and have some fun along the way.

· ·

Put the *fun in the functional part* of your day with these fun learning games.

Count It!

Count the cows, fire hydrants, horses, red cars, blue vans, etc.

Color It!

As your child finds an out-of-state license plate, have him or her color in the corresponding state on a blank map of the United States from the Internet.

Find It!
Find the letters of the alphabet on billboards or signs.

Name It!
Play "name that tune" using familiar children's songs. Start out singing two notes then adding more until the song is identified.

Favorite!
Begin by asking each person to tell his or her favorite color. Let each player have a turn and say another favorite such as a book, movie, game, or amusement park ride.

One last thought...
Don't be afraid to modify the rules or play a new game if your child gets frustrated. Your child will be learning with these games, but the emphasis should be on having fun.

Family
Fun Nights

One of the best things about being a parent is that you get to do all the things you loved as a kid all over again. Get the whole family to join in and have some fun. Try to create a new family tradition by engaging in at least one of the activities below every week.

These activities will bring your family closer together and put smiles on everyone's faces.

Movie Night

Lights, camera, action! Take turns picking one movie to watch as a family once a week. Dim the lights, pop the popcorn, and get into your coziest pajamas. Then, snuggle up and enjoy the movie.

Game Night

Did you have a favorite board game as a child? There are hundreds of board games you can play today. Be sure the game you select is age appropriate and fun! Have your child help you choose the game. If you can't find a game you like, create your own board game!

Scavenger Night Walk

Have each member of your family create a list of five items that can be found on a walk around your community. Swap lists and go together on a family walk at night. Be sure to wear reflective clothing. When you find an item, shine the flashlight on it. The first one to find all the items on his or her list wins!

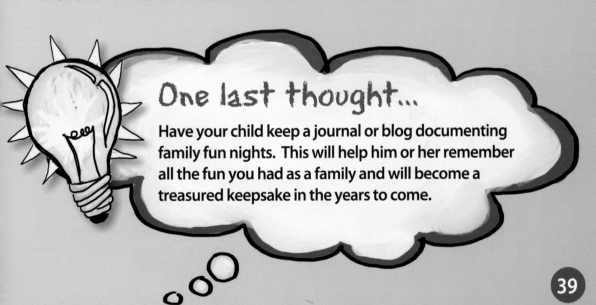

One last thought...

Have your child keep a journal or blog documenting family fun nights. This will help him or her remember all the fun you had as a family and will become a treasured keepsake in the years to come.

Dear Parent,

Thank you for sharing your precious time reading this collection of activities and strategies for integrating learning into everyday living. Guiding your child through first grade can be great fun and have huge rewards. You've made a fine first step by browsing through this handbook.

Keep in mind that this year will fly by. It will seem as if you'd blinked, and suddenly you're getting ready for second grade!

You can make a huge difference during each step of your child's educational journey. Just be sure you enjoy the trip!

Thank you!